The Stable Door

OTHER BOOKS BY JAMES PROTHERO

Theology and C. S. Lewis

Sunbeams and Bottles: the Theology, Thought, and Reading of C. S. Lewis

Simply Mary: Meditations on the Real Life of the Mother of Christ

Gaining a Face: the Romanticism of C. S. Lewis (with Donald T. Williams)

The Form of Faith: Reflections on my Life, Romanticism, Meaning, and the Christian Faith in the Early 21st Century

Sacred Land: Finding Faith in Desert, Mountain, and Forest

Fiction

The Sun is But a Morning Star

Maggie of Long Hollow

The Wind on the Grass

Ana Sanchez and the Coyote Murder

Ana Sanchez and the Hidden Assassins

Ana Sanchez and the Kokopelli Mystery

The Coming of the White Wolf Girl

Darkness Before and Danger's Voice Behind

There Darkness Makes Abode.

The Stable Door

C. S. Lewis, Belief, and the Paradox of Recognition

JAMES PROTHERO

WIPF & STOCK · Eugene, Oregon

THE STABLE DOOR
C. S. Lewis, Belief, and the Paradox of Recognition

Wipf & Stock
An Imprint of Wipf and Stock Publishers
199 W. 8th Ave., Suite 3
Eugene, OR 97401

www.wipfandstock.com

PAPERBACK ISBN: 979-8-3852-5832-1
HARDCOVER ISBN: 979-8-3852-5833-8
EBOOK ISBN: 979-8-3852-5834-5

09/04/25

I am grateful to the C. S. Lewis Company Ltd for granting permission for the use of Lewis quotes in this study.
Mere Christianity by C. S. Lewis copyright© C. S. Lewis Pte. Ltd.
    1942,1943,1944,1952.
Surprised by Joy by C. S. Lewis copyright© C. S. Lewis Pte. Ltd. 1955.
Reflections on the Psalms by C. S. Lewis copyright© C.S.Lewis Pte.
    Ltd.1958.
Letters of CSL vol 3, by C. S. Lewis copyright© C.S.Lewis Pte. Ltd.2007.
    (World excluding USA for *Letters to an American l.ady*)
God in the Dock by C. S. Lewis copyright© C. S. Lewis Pte. Ltd. 1970.
    (World excluding USA)
The Screwtape Letters by C. S. Lewis copyright© C. S. Lewis Pte. Ltd. 1942.
The Problem of Pain by C. S. Lewis copyright© C. S. Lewis Pte. Ltd. 1940.
The Last Battle by C. S. Lewis copyright© C. S. Lewis Pte. Ltd. 1956.'
Christian Reflections by C. S. Lewis copyright© C. S. Lewis Pte. Ltd. 1967.
Christian Reunion by C. S. Lewis copyright© C. S. Lewis Pte. Ltd. 1990.
The World's Last Night and Other Essays by C. S. Lewis copyright© C. S.
    Lewis Pte. Ltd. 1952.

To
Michael Christensen
And all those Northwinders

I am God, and there is no one like me;

I reveal the end from the beginning,

from ancient times I reveal what is to be;

ISAIAH 46: 9–10

Contents

Acknowledgments

I WANT TO THANK first, my partner in Desert Spirit Press, Fr Brad Karelius, who guided and encouraged this project. Also, tremendous thanks go to Hope L'Angevin for her editing acumen. And as always, all I understand about Lewis comes from my blessed exposure to my dear friend, that inestimable Narnia scholar and theologian, Dr Paul F. Ford.

1.

The Emmaus Problem

IN THE GOSPEL OF Luke, chapter 24, verses 13 through 35, we
have a story that appears nowhere else in the New Testament.
Christ has been crucified and buried, and two of his followers,
one named Cleopas, the other unnamed, are retreating from Jerusalem. The reader gets the impression that they have decided
the whole thing is bewildering and dangerous, and their team
spirit is lagging. This Jesus Christ has turned out to be another
letdown. And in this passage, we see the very thing that C. S.
Lewis said convinces him that the Gospel accounts are authentic:
that is, the very personal nature of the narrative and the amateur
errors by the narrator, in this case, Luke.

Luke gives us the kind of details known only to eyewit-
nesses. It's on a Sunday ("first day of the week"); Jesus' exasper-
ated words on slowness to belief are directly quoted, something
only an ear-witness could do. Could the other be Luke himself?
Luke takes pains not to name himself in the Book of Acts, even
though he was obviously with Paul on the latter journeys and
the voyage to Rome. I've always suspected that the detailed nature of the account indicates that the second man on the road
to Emmaus is Luke, whom tradition identifies as a Greek. I've

often wondered if Luke was one of the Greeks who came to Jesus in John 12:20–22.

They are walking to a village called Emmaus. Cleopas and Maybe-Luke are trying to get clear of the mess. The Jewish authorities and the Romans have destroyed the leader of the movement, or so Cleopas and Maybe-Luke think. The Romans, being thorough folk, are not ones to leave loose ends. And mopping up the remnants of Christ's followers, and jailing, or executing them, seems highly likely. Cleopas and Maybe-Luke will take a pass on being mopped up by the Romans. But still they are saddened. We know this from Cleopas' tone as he recites the sad tale of Jesus of Nazareth to the stranger that they walk with. When he finishes, the stranger first scolds them for being slow to believe, and then explains the prophecies in Jewish scripture referring to the Messiah. They are just making traveling conversation, and they get a complete YouTube course on prophesy (minus the internet).

And this is the startling thing for me, and what this book is really about: in the moment with Cleopas and Maybe-Luke, our Lord Jesus Christ expects them to have been somewhat forewarned by the Torah and the Prophets about the events in the life of the Messiah. He *expects them to get it*. His tone is unmistakable. The exclamation is a clear chiding. How slow you are to believe all that the prophets wrote about the Messiah, says the Messiah himself, to those who are not hostile, but his followers. Why were they expected to 'get it'? And what exactly were they expected to get, especially since in Palestine of that day even the Jewish leaders were divided between Pharisee and Sadducee on just how scripture was to be read?

Most Christians today pretty much accept the long-standing Christian explanation of why the Pharisees and Sadducees did not accept the teachings of Jesus Christ. We have Jesus' own critique of these religious leaders of his time, that their ritualism has become disconnected from reality and the most important things. Thus, they "strain a gnat and swallow a camel."[1] We've

1. Matthew 23:24.

also been taught that the Pharisees, and indeed, Jesus' own followers, expected a military Messiah to drive off the Romans.
Plus, the New Testament accuses the Pharisees of being jealous
of Jesus.[2] Certainly the Pharisees and Sadducees expected any
real Messiah who showed up, would be one of *their* party. And
they were angered and stunned that this Messiah not only did
not approve of them, but that he severely criticized their prized
interpretation of how to be a good Jew.

And yet. And yet. And yet, Jesus expects Cleopas and
Maybe-Luke to have got this. Nor is this the first instance of
Jesus rebuking people for not thinking straight about faith and
scripture. In Mark 12:24–27 Jesus demolishes the Sadducees
and their argument over the resurrection with a well-reasoned
and unanswerable argument. In the process he gives them an
unmistakable verbal slap by telling them that they don't know
the scriptures, which reminds us of his rebuke of Cleopas and
Maybe-Luke. Messianic prophecy and scriptural understanding
may be for us an academic fire-swamp, with scholars buzzing
about it like maddened bees. But while on Earth, Jesus Christ
speaks as if there is one reasonable interpretation to the whole
thing, and those that don't get it stand the risk of being told
off for their rational failings. If we look through the Gospels
with these issues in mind, we find there are as well, a number
of Gospel incidents where Jesus out-argues the Pharisees and
rebukes them for having gotten it wrong. We may be inclined
to be generous with others who have a different interpretation
of all these matters, but the fact is, Our Lord was anything but
tolerant of what he saw as bad reasoning about scripture. This
is probably a large part of the reason that the people of Jesus'
time were amazed that he spoke with authority.[3] There is no
academic dithering in Jesus Christ. And class dunces will be
called out by God incarnate for shoddy thinking and given a
time-out in the corner.

2. Mark 15:10.

3. Matthew 7:28–29.

Ok. So, getting it correct was and is important. Still, we know, at least on one level, that Jesus' ability to perform miracles was limited by the ability of the people around him to believe.[4] Yet the other, and deeper issue, and perhaps the most thorny one, is that Old Testament prophecy regarding the Messiah is so ambiguous, that there is a small industry of books on it from the Christian perspective alone, not to mention the Jewish scholarship that is not inclined to take Jesus' view of what scripture means. Our first impression is that Our Lord is perhaps unfairly taking two of his followers to task for not finding the intended meaning in some ancient and ambiguous texts, which would hardly be reasonable. Rather, a more sensible reading is that it seems that a certain attitude, or level of belief, is necessary to understand how Old Testament prophecy applies to Jesus of Nazareth. Let him who has ears to hear, indeed.[5] Cleopas and Maybe-Luke get a gentle scolding, not so much because they missed the correct interpretation, but because they had witnessed the power of Christ, the miracles, including perhaps the resurrection of Lazarus. Their belief should have opened up these ambiguous passages in Jewish scripture and should have given them, as it were, Jesus Christ's midrash—thus God's midrash on Jewish prophecy. Talk about straight from the horse's mouth. And though we all wish Luke had written down every word of what the Lord said, the more important thing here is that you have to be open to belief first, before you can see and understand. This, of course, goes all the way back to St. Augustine.

Descartes goes out the window here. Like Cleopas and Maybe-Luke, you must *recognize* Jesus first to believe in him and to understand what was written about him in prophecy. The whole process works backwards of what we would expect, in our post-cartesian age. With firm belief, all the clues come clear. This is somewhat like the experience of reaching the end of an Agatha Christie novel. All the clues we missed jump out at us when we come to believe the keystone truth. In fact, this is

4. Mark 6:4–13.

5. Matthew 11:15.

what I call Recognition, that is, the mystery of how some people come to believe in Christ in the manner of recognizing something they have always suspected, and in a sense they always knew down deep. I will not pretend to completely understand this, or even come close to grasping why this is so. Like many things involved in the tenuous link between God and humanity, it ultimately is a mystery. But the fact is that our experience, and our exploring of scripture are full of such instances, and not just the Emmaus event.

So, this is the central concept of this book. Recognition is believing, or at least the willingness to believe, that precedes seeing and proof. And my Agatha Christie analogy was apt, because that's what it feels like to have what I'm calling the Emmaus experience. We almost knew and now that we see, all the clues we didn't get jump out at us. Part of the power of Lewis' *Narnia Chronicles* is that you feel like you know Aslan personally, the very moment he appears, and the sensation only gets stronger with further reading. This is another example of what I call Recognition.

We can speculate endlessly on whether Cleopas and Maybe-Luke did not recognize Jesus while they were walking because Jesus intended them to not recognize him right away. The passage seems to indicate that interpretation. But it seems more likely to me that belief is something that only happens to the prepared mind. Maybe they were always able to recognize him as they walked, but their own prejudice, their own conviction that the Romans had destroyed him, kept them from recognizing the Master as he walked and talked beside them.

This for me is a far more important take-away than Jesus' reading of Old Testament messianic prophecy (though I'd give a whole lot to know what he said). Cleopas and Maybe-Luke were not ready to recognize Jesus because they thought he was dead. Things like this happen to us all the time. We expect things to fall out in a certain way and miss the obvious right in front of us, because we were not prepared to believe it was there.

But there is one more often-overlooked element to this story, and it is this: we might look at what Jesus had to say to Cleopas and Maybe-Luke not so much as a Divine Midrash, though it was certainly that. But that it was what they needed to hear to knock loose their jammed ability to believe. For Luke as narrator, this is obviously far more important than the details of Jesus' interpretation of Jewish scripture. They were able to believe just about the same time as they recognized Jesus. This may seem a small coincidence, but I am certain in fact that this is the whole point. Perhaps that is why the moment they recognized him, he vanished. The work was done and there was nothing more to say. We can't know for sure, since Jesus did not often share why he did things the way he did with his disciples. Though usually when he did share, they didn't get it. Look at Peter when Jesus reveals that he is going to Jerusalem to die.[6]

Over the decades of my own scriptural reading, I've seen this pattern of the vital importance of Recognition again and again. So, imagine my complete surprise when, as I was discovering the writing and thought of C. S. Lewis, I discovered that the matter was central to his own thinking as well. In this volume I want to explore the original and surprising ideas Lewis held about what I have called Recognition, and their bearing on this whole problem of Emmaus, of being expected to recognize Christ in the prophecies.

Lewis wrote to the person who wanted to be a believing Christian, but found too many logical and/or practical objections. So, this book will be more than a study of Lewis. In the spirit of his own writing, it will be about this uncanny sense that some of us have when God approaches us through circumstances that are just too coincidental.

Our Lord had a lot to say on this subject in all four of the Gospels. Yet I have known people who seem to think that either faith, or agnosticism, or even atheism, are somehow obvious and self-proving. On the other hand I have known those who think that simply announcing the Gospel of Christ around the world

6. Matthew 16:21–23.

might cause the whole planet to follow the Lord. But Jesus Christ himself did not believe this.[7] Nor did Lewis. Belief is far more complex a thing. In any case, this immediately throws us into the dark and stormy seas of theological debate. Nothing for it. In we go.

7. Matthew 7:13–14.

2.

Theoretical Theology and Negative Capability

C. S. Lewis worked hard throughout most of his life not to cause any more division in the Body of Christ. Yet, that did not stop him from in various places indicating that he believed that when the judgment finally comes, many will enter into Aslan's Country that we did not expect, and many we did expect, will not. He illustrates this vividly, echoing Matthew 7: 21–23, in the scene where Aslan stands at the stable door overlooking Narnia, in *The Last Battle*. And for Lewis, the crucial moment that decides this is not having had an "altar-call conversion," or not. Nor is it a test of one's dogma. It is the question of how one responds to Aslan (Jesus) when one comes to him face to face. This scene in *The Last Battle* has stirred controversy, primarily from those who hold that having an altar-call, or some form of rather obvious, rapid, dogmatic, and visible conversion to faith in Jesus Christ is the only way to avoid Hell and go to Heaven. Usually, adherence to a particular form of Protestant dogma is equally important. And sadly, the avoidance of Hell is usually the big selling point in this sort of theology, a left-over from the largely Medieval idea that it was good practice to try to scare people into the church. The Puritans were tremendously guilty of this, as was the Medieval Catholic Church. Yet it was always a deceptive and destructive practice, and something in hindsight that sensible Christians can only look back on with regret.

As I have said above, I believe in this matter of Recognition, Lewis is not clearing away blockage for people who misunderstand, as he does throughout *Mere Christianity*. Here is one of the few places I can think of where Lewis is exploring an area of theology, in which he has no final answer nor authoritative tradition of consensus in Christian belief to or from which he can explain and appeal. Here, Lewis' theology is theoretical. This is similar to his exploration of petitionary prayer, in *Christian Reflections*, an essay at the end of which he admits he has no answer. Though there is no one essay on Recognition, I think for Lewis, as with petitionary prayer, he explored it to a large degree as a problem without an answer. But explore it, he did. Any sharp reader, and probably almost all theologians at this point, are thinking, "Oh no. Prothero is going into the 'Fire Swamp' of predestination." I think *The Princess Bride* allusion might well be apt, but yes, so I am. I'm probably going to unwisely venture into a few others as well. But first, Negative Capability.

NEGATIVE CAPABILITY

Before I launch into some of the philosophical and theological problems, I think I need to define one aspect of the intellectual space that C. S. Lewis lived in. He is both claimed by religious conservatives, and admired by religious liberals, and yet, as I argued extensively in my previous book[1], he really belongs to neither one. And understanding to what intellectual direction Lewis adheres will make those straining to pigeon-hole him as a liberal or a conservative realize how ultimately futile all such attempts are. And if the reader can grasp Lewis' Negative

---

1. *Sunbeams and Bottles: the Theology, Thought, and Reading of C. S. Lewis.* Winged Lion Press, 2022.

Capability, they may more clearly understand the nature of the rest I wish to impart.

So here I am doing something rare: I am applying the thought processes inherent to the study of English literature, and textual criticism, to matters of theology. It seems an odd and perhaps mistaken approach until one realizes that this is exactly what C. S. Lewis himself did so excellently. Lewis himself was a man of the Creeds: Nicene and Apostles'. As I argued in my previous book, he was an ecclesiastical "originalist," to borrow the term from US Constitution controversy, and believed in basic assertions common to the undivided church of the early centuries and best expressed in the Nicene Creed. This separates him from what he himself called "Fundamentalists" in his *Reflection on the Psalms*.[2] Lewis defines these people as those who, in regard to the Bible and dogma, " . . . should have preferred, an unrefracted light giving us ultimate truth in systematic form—something we could have tabulated and memorised and relied on like the multiplication table." Thus, according to Lewis, fundamentalism, of any kind, is a systematized structure that pretends to answer all questions and leaves no doubts. Lewis did not believe in any such thing, though his belief in the objective fact of the assertions of the Nicene Creed was rock solid. But Lewis on the other hand rejected what I have labeled the Neo-Deist form of belief, what he called "Liberal Christianity." I have coined my own term, 'Neo-Deism' because Lewis' term "Liberal Christianity" can imply that the set of beliefs that Lewis objected to had something to do with American liberal politics today, which is not necessarily true. Lewis defined "Liberal Christianity" as an attempt to strip the miraculous and supernatural out of Christian belief. And Lewis believed this to be futile. For me, this so-called Liberal Christianity seems to be a second wave of the skepticism of the late 1700s that congealed into Deism. In both cases, the primary energy of Deism, new and old, was to strip God of any agency, and to conform the tatters of Christianity after doing so, to a materialistic world view.

2. Lewis, *Reflection on the Psalms*, 112.

As he does in so many places, Lewis avoids extremes and steers a middle course. He resists the fundamentalist urge to have all questions answered and all behaviors and issues neatly systematized in an easily referenced web of cultural custom and biblical interpretation. He likewise resists the gassy subjectivism of Neo-Deism, that all too often either degenerates into the default setting for the human mind, as Lewis saw it: pantheism, or perhaps to agnosticism. And he does this by holding firmly to the objective Creeds, and leaving much of the rest to a kind of Negative Capability. But let me define that term.

In a December 1817 letter to his brothers, the English poet, John Keats, writes:

> I had not a dispute but a disquisition with Dilke, on various subjects; several things dovetailed in my mind, & at once it struck me, what quality went to form a Man of Achievement especially in Literature & which Shakespeare possessed so enormously—I mean Negative Capability, that is when man is capable of being in uncertainties, Mysteries, doubts, without any irritable reaching after fact & reason.[3]

As I have already argued in two books, Lewis was completely Romantic in his thinking and was well-read in Keats. And what Keats here is describing, for those readers not accustomed to 19th century prose, is a state of mind in which one accepts that there are mysteries and unknowns that we cannot reach to. Our knowledge of the universe will always be vastly incomplete. For the record, this would include our theological knowledge. And an "irritable reaching after fact" will not improve that situation. To Keats, as to Lewis, we mistake our understanding of ourselves when with construct systems and postulate answers to matters we cannot fathom, what Lewis calls "Fundamentalism." In doing so, we are erring by that irritable reaching after fact and reason when we do not have the ability to answer such questions. We know only so much. Beyond that is the unknown, and no system

---

3. Keats, *Poetical Works*, 43.

of ours will ever be adequate. I see this as a kind of humility, and I dare say both Keats and Lewis did as well.

But because the chance of misunderstanding is so vast, let me state unequivocally that Negative Capability is *not* another kind of relativism, or subjectivism. Lewis is clearly on the record as opposing both those things. And what Lewis knows, he knows. It's Lewis who tells us that the only reason to become a Christian is because you believe the Carpenter from Nazareth was really God visiting us. This is basic fact. Yet, that certainty, and Lewis' certainty of many Christian truths, co-exists with his humility, his knowing that neither we nor the Bible have the ready-to-hand answers to every question. It is that humility that Keats had in allowing for his own ignorance. That then is Negative Capability. And this is what allows Keats to explore poetic thoughts and ideas. And this same Negative Capability allows Lewis to grapple with such monsters as predestination, free-will, petitionary prayer, the 'sin of encore', and Recognition, and yet keep his solid footing on the Creeds.

Lewis is probing into unknown theological territory. He is not stating these things with the certainty that he stated credal elements in his *Mere Christianity*. This is theoretical theology. He is like a story writer taking us into a work of premise fiction. "What if . . . ?" he says. If you can grasp this Negative Capability of Lewis', you will be able to understand what comes next.

3.

The Seeing Eye and the Stable Door

MY FRIEND AND PARTNER in Desert Spirit Press, Fr. Brad Karelius, points out in his *Desert Spirit Places*, as well as other books
of his, that we as a culture are "post-Enlightenment." We have
a Cartesian point of view and even if we're thorough-going
Christians, we tend to take almost a materialistic point of view,
believing nothing but what science proves, outside of our step
forward into faith. Fr. Brad points out that as Hamlet told Horatio, "There are more things in heaven and Earth, Horatio, / Than
are dreamt of in your philosophy."[1]

So, we are a people who are skeptical of the supernatural
by cultural training, in a way our ancestors would have found
bewildering. Lewis confronts this directly in an essay titled "The
Seeing Eye." In the essay, Lewis takes on the assertion by Russian
cosmonauts that they went into space and didn't see God. Lewis
dismisses this as foolishness, as any god that lived in a region
and was always visible, was not the God that Christianity is talking about. He then does something he does in at least two other
places, and compares God to a novelist or a playwright. He says
that this thick-headed statement by the Cosmonauts is analo-
gous to Hamlet expecting to see Shakespeare. As Shakespeare is

1. Act 1, sc. 5

everywhere and yet never seen in his play, so God is everywhere and never seen in our lives. He concludes "To some, God is discoverable everywhere; to others, nowhere. Those that do not find Him on earth are unlikely to find Him in space."[2]

What is curious about this is that across the corpus of his work, Lewis is certain of the Divinity of Christ. And yet here in this essay, Lewis is uncertain that something as basic as the fact that a chair in front of us is really all that simple, when we start to break it down to the molecular and atomic levels. To Lewis, of course, the answer is that God is the ultimate reality, and following Plato, all the realities we see are mere imitations of the Ultimate Reality in God and in the Forms. This would make the Cosmonauts missing a view of God from Earth orbit, frankly absurd. As Lewis concludes, God is everywhere and even earth is already in space, so the idea that we don't see him because he's floating out in space, is equally laughable.

However, this raises a larger question that though he does it more subtly, Lewis confronts in a unique way. For though the materialist and cartesian assumptions behind the Cosmonauts' scoffing are something Lewis has dismissed at length in his book, *Miracles*, there is a larger question of belief looming here. Is belief itself a good thing? After all, the world is full of charlatans and Elmer Gantrys. In dismissing a materialist skepticism and franchising belief without positive material proof, are we opening ourselves up to delusion? To being suckered? And secondly, with all the religious options out there, how can Christianity seriously make a claim to be the sole truth and the other faiths to be lies?

The first issue involves the possible dangers of abandoning a Cartesian skepticism for openness to belief. Secondly, I want to further explore this problem by addressing what I call the argument from variety. The first question is certainly a valid one in this world plagued with lies and liars. The safest position has always been the confused shrug of agnosticism. But there are two problems with this: first, I have never met anyone, or heard

2. Lewis, *Christian Reflections*, 171.

of anyone who became Christian as the result of pure logic. It is always a combination of the lessons and feelings of personal experience, a metaphorical understanding, and something else beyond human understanding, including mine. And I find that as the materialist can neither prove nor disprove God and the need for faith, neither can the Christian prove nor disprove those things. We're all taking a tremendous gamble, except for the agnostic who lives in perpetual doubt. I know atheists who claim to be only doing the rational thing, and yet I find that none of them that I've encountered seem to be able to rest easy in this assumption. They often find that they possess the inexorable need to evangelize, as if they needed the concurrence of all their fellow humans in order to feel settled in their belief. Again, to paraphrase Hamlet's mother, "Methinks [they] doth protest too much." Actually, most of the atheists I know are atheist not because their extreme faith in what is often called Logical Positivism. For anyone uncertain, Logical Positivism is the belief that one can only believe what is positively proved. I know one atheist who thinks this way, but he is an outlier. And Logical Positivism as a formal philosophy was short-lived simply because one cannot positively prove Logical Positivism. At its heart is an assumption, and therefore, a contradiction.

But I find many more people are atheists because they've experienced tragedy in their lives, and God didn't pop in and save the situation. I am not mocking anyone's valid experience of suffering here. No one escapes pain. C. S. Lewis knew it at age 9, as his mother died of cancer. And God did not miraculously heal her. As he grew older, he became an atheist, I believe much in part, because of this. And this pattern is more common than not. Only a fool pretends to know why God allows particular suffering to visit particular people. C. S. Lewis may have written that pain is God's "megaphone to rouse a deaf world,"[3] but he never attempted to explain why his mother and his wife both died in agony, of cancer. This again, is his Negative Capability, this leaving of the incomprehensible without "any irritable reaching after

---

3. Lewis, *Problem of Pain*, 58.

fact & reason." The argument from suffering is unanswerable in the specific. Even Lewis' *A Grief Observed* acknowledges that. For those who do have faith, like Jesus at Gethsemane, they accept that the will of God may be to allow for the horrible, unthinkable thing to happen and offer it up to God in resignation. Thus, most atheists I have encountered are not dispassionately arriving at a logical conclusion so much as responding to incomprehensible suffering.

In terms of popularity, when it's not the argument from meaningless suffering, what I find to be often the argument against faith is what I call the Argument from Variety. It runs something like this: there are so many religions out there making so many conflicting claims, that they therefore must all be false. Of course this is easily demonstrated to be a fallacious argument, as we might postulate ten men standing on the aft deck of the Titanic, nine of whom are coming up with wild theories as to what is happening and the tenth claiming that the ship is sinking. The multiplicity of claims does not automatically prove them all to be false. However, most people are not trained in logic and find that a multitude of claims breeds skepticism in their minds, as they are accustomed to being bombarded by advertising which really is made up of multiple, manipulative lies. Still, that does not mean that being told a truth is impossible. We are all gambling. And the important thing is that belief is not inevitable in any way; it is always a choice.

And Lewis' way of presenting this choice is controversial. Let's get back to the image from *The Last Battle* of the stable door. Before the Narnia series even began, Lewis introduced an idea in the opening of the second book of *Mere Christianity*, where he departs from the American Fundamentalist understanding in a large way. He states that before he was a Christian, he had to believe that all religions were wrong, or that once becoming a Christian, one had to believe that all religions other than Christianity were wrong and Christianity right. But Lewis clearly states that the religions of the world all contain elements of truth, even though Christ is the Ultimate Truth. "If you are a Christian, you are free to think that all these religions, even the queerest ones, contain at least some hint of the truth."[4]

This flies in the face of altar-call-or-Hell theology. Nor is Lewis in any detectable way reluctant that his statement is offensive to that school of theology. What really roils the waters is when one holds these statements up to the previously mentioned, all-important scene of the judgement at the stable door in *The Last Battle*. And the culprit that makes so many Lewis admirers who are American Fundamentalists uncomfortable is the scene in Aslan's Country with the Calormene officer named Emeth.

In brief, Emeth is an officer in the force come to claim Narnia for the Tisroc, and a life-long worshipper of the demon-god, Tash. Aslan confronts him and because all that Emeth has done has been morally upright, and more importantly, in longing for the love of the Creator God, Aslan accepts that service and claims it for his own. Lewis marks this passage with two of his ideas: first, that all that is done in Aslan's (Christ's) name that is evil, is service to Tash (or perhaps, Satan); and all that is good that is done in Tash's name is actual service to Aslan. The second point is something Lewis repeats in several places, that all find what they truly seek. This latter point plays to the idea of Recognition.

Before I part with the stable door entirely, I would like to point out one thing that is certain to annoy American Fundamentalists even more, and that has probably been overlooked. Some of these folks take small comfort in Aslan making only one exception for Emeth. That seems to bolster their altar-call concept. Yet, if you read the account carefully, Emeth is not the only Calormene to apparently have been accepted into Aslan's Country on such terms. For in the chapter "Night Falls on Narnia" every sentient creature in the Narnian world comes streaming up to the Stable Door, where they either love Aslan and enter, or hate him and turn away into darkness. Lewis nowhere tells us that only Narnians enter. He does tell us that some of them turn away, losing their status as talking animals, their status as "hnau,"

4. Lewis, *Mere Christianity*, 35.

as Lewis calls persons of other species in *Out of the Silent Planet*.
They are all described as "creatures," and some enter Aslan's
Country while others do not. Lewis' list of creatures includes
"talking beasts, dwarfs, satyrs, fauns, giants, *Calormenes* [emphasis mine], men from Archenland, Monopods, and strange
unearthly things from the remote islands or the unknown western lands."[5] So, we have to conclude that Emeth is just one of
many Calormenes who enter Aslan's Country.

This whole scene is uncomfortable to those who want an
altar-call Christianity, and knowable list of who is saved. I believe in part that this knowable salvation appeals mainly because
of the Fundamentalist emphasis on having the correct theology.
But though Lewis elsewhere tells us that error to some degree
disables, salvation in this fairy tale of Narnia is represented by
the Love of God, and not having correct theological opinions.

Having said that, I think I should quote Lewis at length
here, from his essay on "Christian Reunion," lest anyone think
that I'm arguing for a relativistic Lewis.

> That the spiritual life transcends both intelligence and
> morality, we are probably all agreed. But I suppose it
> transcends them as poetry transcends grammar, and
> does not merely exclude them as algebra excludes
> grammar. . . . To the very last, when two people differ
> in doctrine, logic proclaims that though both might be
> in error, it is impossible for both to be right. And error
> always to some extent disables.[6]

So, here we see that Lewis himself is cautious. Error to some
extent disables. Error matters. Christ being the "way, the truth,
and the life" matters supremely. Paul Ford, perhaps the most expert scholar on Narnia that we have, in a talk I attended, pointed
out that when Emeth discovers Aslan, the Lion is between two
great rocks. The metaphor implies that there is no way around
Aslan. Indeed, at the stable door, there is definitely no way around
Aslan. Every creature is confronted and makes a choice.

5. Lewis, *The Last Battle*, 144.
6. Lewis, *Christian Reunion*, 21.

If all this seems too exploratory, too uncertain for some readers, I submit that this is because Lewis here *is* exploring. In his Negative Capability, he is feeling his way forward, and his uncertainty is revealed in that he placed this matter firmly in his fantasy novels, but nowhere in his apologetics, beyond the brief statement of the possibility of truth being in non-Christian religions in *Mere Christianity*. And this is because what I have called Recognition, as I have said before and now say again firmly, is ultimately a mystery. Lewis is not certain about it. No one can be. This is why he doesn't push the argument to some logical extreme. It would only darken counsel for those considering the leap of faith. Lewis is too wise and too aware of his reader and audience to dump a deep mystery on those who are just considering seriously the claims of Christ.

Indeed, I have come to believe that the doctrines of predestination and universalism are both equal and opposite extremes as well as oversimplifications that attempt to define the mystery of Recognition. That will be the matter for the next chapter. In my view they are both instances of "out of the pan and into the fire," that is, they bracket Recognition without successfully explaining it. They exaggerate one aspect of the mystery in the vain attempt to solve it. But in fact, they invite their own rational and theological objections. And they darken counsel. What's more, I think I can show that rejection of both predestination and universalism is what CS Lewis believed.

4.

Predestination, Universalism, and other Fire-Swamps

I AM CONVINCED THAT Recognition, whatever else it might be, is pure grace. And that, sadly, drags us into the Fire-Swamps of predestination and universalism. Let's start with Lewis on the record. In a letter to Mary Van Deusen, Lewis wrote in 1952: "All that Calvinist question—Free Will & Predestination, is to my mind undiscussable, insoluble. . . . I suspect it is really a meaningless question."[1] I have pulled out the most important parts of this passage, but the rest is very informative. Lewis cobles together a list of paradoxical scriptural 'contradictions' that are endemic to the free will versus predestination debate, all of which are unanswerable.

He goes much deeper in a letter a year later to Emily McLay. There he points out that New Testament passages indicating free-will and choice are mixed with passages that speak in terms of predestination. He warns that we cannot contradict one part of scripture with another. He adds that whatever St Paul may have meant:

---

1. Lewis, *Collected Letters of C. S. Lewis*, 3:237–38.

. . . we must not reject the parable of the sheep and the goats. (Matt. XXV. 30—46). There, you see there is nothing about Predestination or even about Faith—all depends on works.[2]

He goes on to argue that the urge to simplify all this to predestination is a natural and logical impulse "to turn this personal experience into a general rule. 'All conversions depend on God's choice.'"[3] Then he warns against generalizations where we don't have all the facts. He advocates we do like scientists do, and where the evidence is inconsistent, we hold the inconsistent facts and admit freely that we cannot reconcile them. This is, in fact, a nice short description of Negative Capability that Lewis is advocating here. In the following paragraph Lewis states it plainly.

The real inter-relation between God's omnipotence and Man's freedom is something we can't find out. Looking at the Sheep & the Goats [in Matthew 25: 31—46] every man can be quite sure that every kind act he does will be accepted by Christ. Yet, equally, we all do feel sure that all the good in us comes from Grace. We have to leave it at that.[4]

And if this weren't enough. In Letter 27, Screwtape explains that the human confusion over predestination is that we invariably imagine that God is locked in time as we are. But God is, in Lewis' view, too real to be parceled out like we are. For God, there is only present tense. God never "foreknew" that you would do this or that. He knows it. One image, a metaphor, that has worked for me is the wagon wheel: we live our lives running around the rim, spoke to spoke. God is in the hub and all the spokes of your or my life touch him together in one. I'm tempted to say 'one moment', but there again, I'd be picturing God as inside time. As we discussed above, God's relation to us is more like Shakespeare's relation to Hamlet. Shakespeare equally

2. Lewis, *Collected Letters of C. S. Lewis*, 354.

3. Lewis, *Collected Letters of C. S. Lewis*, 355.

4. Lewis, *Collected Letters of C. S. Lewis*, 355.

accesses all parts of the play. Only Hamlet must march through to his weary fate, moment by moment. For all we know, perhaps Shakespeare wrote the final scene first. Of course, this metaphor breaks down when we think of Shakespeare operating in time—the order in which he wrote the various scenes in *Hamlet*. It is tremendously difficult for us to imagine God operating outside time. In fact, I believe it's impossible. We cannot wrap our minds around it. As with predestination, as Lewis advised above, we should accept it and then "leave it at that."

The opposite vision is universalism. This appeals to those of us who can't believe a loving God would throw sinners into Hell. But as much as he believed in a loving God and agreed with George MacDonald's theology, Lewis was no universalist. It's a rather long explanation of Lewis' take on Hell. I haven't space to go into all of that here. However, I will say that Lewis' central concept of Hell is that "the doors to Hell are locked from the inside."[5] No one who wants love, God, and joy, will be turned away. We see this in the stable door scene where all sorts of creatures are welcomed in the moment that they recognize Aslan. There are no dogma tests. The other thing to know is that when Lewis does portray Hell, it is not the ridiculous image of devils in red tights, a sad leftover from the Puritans and the Middle Ages. Lewis' hell is a gray city where everyone is constantly concerned about their own dignity, narcissism, desires, and wants, and hate everyone else, whom they see as problems. With free will, a person can insist on these things above love, and to do so is to be in Hell. So Hell is not the whim of a wrathful and petty Jehovah, petulantly lobbing lightning bolts at naughty children. Hell is a prison we create for our own souls. Lewis, in discussing the concept and George MacDonald's near-universalism, addresses the assertion that all people will be saved. He simply asks whether that is with their will—or not?[6]

Here again, Lewis argues briefly, but his true theological concepts are portrayed in the Narnia tales, and other fiction.

5. Lewis, *Problem of Pain*, 81.

6. Lewis, *Problem of Pain*, 75.

As my title implies, the central image that Lewis gives us is that humble stable on a forgotten hill in Narnia which becomes the Door to Aslan's Country. Everything is in those scenes: primarily, the acceptance of all who do something like recognize Aslan and love him and are therefore invited into Aslan's Country; the inability of the dwarves who cannot get outside their own skepticism. And, of course, there's the Emeth scene, as if the judgment at the stable door wasn't enough.

Even more, there's the scene in *Till We Have Faces* where Psyche is telling Orual about the moment she first saw the God of the West Wind before her. She tells Orual that though the god only looked vaguely human, Psyche herself only felt shame over her mortal shape in the god's presence. She had been praying to the gods to end her misery, when this god who had demanded her finally appears to her. The calling of the god happens in concert with the calling of the mortal. And if I took the time, I could find more such scenes. Lewis probes the mystery of Recognition in fantasy fiction, but will not apply logic to it. It is a mystery. Predestination doesn't satisfy reason to one side; universalism doesn't satisfy reason to the other.

Recognition is that dynamic and unanchored position between these extremes.

And I'm afraid that is as close as I can come to a definition. But I'm bothered by the fact that it's a negative definition—it tells us the outer borders of Recognition but not the internal content. Yet, again, that is the area of mystery. I think Our Lord himself says it best in a metaphor. There is no literal language about it, precisely because it is beyond the grasp of the human mind. In John 10: 27, 28 it reads:

> My sheep hear my voice. I know them, and they follow
> me. I give them eternal life, and they will never perish.
> No one will snatch them out of my hand.

Lewis again presents this in story, by the scene of Aslan standing at the stable door, and every creature in the Narnian world having one of two reactions as they look at him. Likewise,

Aslan knows everything about the life of Emeth, and Emeth, though he believes Aslan is his enemy, recognizes him, just as surely as Aslan recognizes Emeth. If I may borrow from the language of the scripture above, Emeth is one of the sheep that hears Aslan's voice and knows and follows him, even though he has always imagined that he served Tash.

So, the best I can do for a definition, again, is that Recognition is that dynamic and unanchored position between the extremes of predestination and universalism.

5.

Lewis and Invincible Ignorance

BUT WHY IS EMETH not blamed for his devoted worship of
Tash? In short, he is excused as a case of "invincible ignorance."
This sounds like an insult, but it is not. The concept of Invincible Ignorance has a long historical precedent. The church
father, Origen, discussed the concept in his *Homilies on Joshua*
around 250 CE. St Thomas Aquinas mentions it in his discussions on sin in the *Summa Theologica*. Pope Pius IX includes
it in his 1854 document, *Singulari Quadam*, and also in his
1863 *Quanto Conficiamur Moerore*. So, the concept has a long
history in Roman Catholic theology.

As I argued in my study, *Sunbeams and Bottles*, Lewis really
knew very little about the Roman Catholic Church and its theology after the Renaissance. And I have yet to find that he read
Cardinal Newman so far as to have read the *Essay on the Development of Doctrine*, though he read much of other Newman
texts. The discussions that led to Vatican II, which took place in
his final years and beyond his death, were entirely overlooked by
Lewis, so that he would not have been familiar with the text in
Lumen Gentium, section 16, which reads:

> 16. Finally, those who have not yet received the Gospel
> are related in various ways to the people of God. In the

first place we must recall the people to whom the testament and the promises were given and from whom Christ was born according to the flesh. On account of their fathers this people remains most dear to God, for God does not repent of the gifts He makes nor of the calls He issues. But the plan of salvation also includes those who acknowledge the Creator. In the first place amongst these there are the Muslims, who, professing to hold the faith of Abraham, along with us adore the one and merciful God, who on the last day will judge mankind. Nor is God far distant from those who in shadows and images seek the unknown God, for it is He who gives to all men life and breath and all things, and as Saviour wills that all men be saved. Those also can attain to salvation who through no fault of their own do not know the Gospel of Christ or His Church, yet sincerely seek God and moved by grace strive by their deeds to do His will as it is known to them through the dictates of conscience. Nor does Divine Providence deny the helps necessary for salvation to those who, without blame on their part, have not yet arrived at an explicit knowledge of God and with His grace strive to live a good life. Whatever good or truth is found amongst them is looked upon by the Church as a preparation for the Gospel. She knows that it is given by Him who enlightens all men so that they may finally have life. But often men, deceived by the Evil One, have become vain in their reasonings and have exchanged the truth of God for a lie, serving the creature rather than the Creator. Or some there are who, living and dying in this world without God, are exposed to final despair. Wherefore to promote the glory of God and procure the salvation of all of these, and mindful of the command of the Lord, "Preach the Gospel to every creature," the Church fosters the missions with care and attention.

This is the current Catholic understanding of invincible ignorance. Remarkably, it is very consonant with the whole Emeth scene in *The Last Battle*. How exactly the Catholic concept may have influenced the Emeth scene is impossible to say for sure. But I am convinced that Lewis knew nothing of 19th and 20th century developments in Catholic theology. My guess is that the Emeth scene was a product of Lewis' imagination in total ignorance of Catholic theology. It is possible that Tolkien, or Havard, or Griffiths, or others of Lewis' Catholic friends may have mentioned it, but there is no evidence for this. And given Lewis' stubborn refusal to Griffiths to discuss Catholic theology, I doubt Lewis ever heard of the concept that was growing during his lifetime and found expression in the Vatican II Council.

Lewis' position on this concept of Invincible Ignorance differs somewhat from the official pronouncements of the Catholic Church. The Catholic definition also includes "vincible" ignorance, which might be defined as the stubborn refusal not to know the truth when one has the opportunity. Vincible ignorance does not morally excuse a lack of faith. Lewis does not venture into this area. For Lewis, the incentive comes from another quarter.

Lewis himself, as is well-illustrated in his *Surprised by Joy*, came to Christianity slowly, reluctantly, and by a largely intellectual path. So, like many of his readers, he looked to outside sources to eliminate roadblocks to faith. The prominent placement of his above-quoted statement from *Mere Christianity*, about Christians being able to believe that there is truth in other religions, highlights the importance to Lewis of a mind opened to all truth, and all nuances in coming to faith in Christ. One of the features of what Lewis would call a more fundamentalist concept of faith would be the rejection of any thought not coming from the immediate church body and its sacred dogma of faith. Though, as quoted above, Lewis feels that all error disables, he is all too aware of the bitterly comic tragedy of church groups loudly condemning others to Hell who do not exactly share in the minute points of their theology. Lewis knows that the Spirit blows where he wills. And that I believe, and not any doctrinal speculation, nor exposure to Catholic doctrine, is the genesis of the Emeth scene in *The Last Battle*.

Furthermore, I believe for Lewis, that is the point. I have written novels, and as a novelist, scenes most often just pop out of my head unbidden, or so it feels. Other fiction writers assure me that they have the same experience. It's actually a good sign for a novelist if the novel seems to take on a life of its own and leave the novelist behind. So, let us *not* imagine that Lewis is carefully calculating out the Emeth scene. This is pouring out of his subconscious in the form of imagery. And ringing in the back of Lewis' mind as he's hand-writing out the Emeth scene is not only the thought that the Spirit goes where he will, but the words of Christ himself that "my sheep hear my voice." And that, simply said, is Recognition.

Lewis here is being the theoretical theologian. And the primary, driving thought is that Lewis cannot believe that God Almighty would be unjust in his judgement. This conviction is the origin point for Lewis' theoretical foray in *The Last Battle* with Emeth. He will not explore all the implications. He seems to know that he has taken to theological wings and is not in touch with the ground. He is content to soar for just a bit. But, he's not going to put this short flight of theology into his apologetic writings. Yet, he is convinced that God is just, and God's sheep know his voice. Lewis is willing to leap just that far, and no more, into an image of Recognition.

6.

Is Theology Poetry? Recognition and Confirmation Bias

IN A TALK GIVEN to the Socratic Club on 6 November 1944, Lewis gave a response to the question "Is theology poetry?" Lewis spends the beginning of the talk defining the question, which could mean at very least, two different things. In the talk, he manages to combine several concepts that he wrote about in other essays. But the part I want to focus on is when he parses the question to mean: 'Is Christian theology merely poetry?' Because here he is fearlessly wandering into the part of the battlefield dominated by the forces of the Giant named Freud. If this sounds like I'm getting carried away with metaphor and personal symbol, it is not so. This is exactly how Lewis allegorizes this Freud in *The Pilgrim's Regress*.

To put the concept in more current terms, Lewis is addressing the accusation against Christian belief, that it is mere "wish fulfillment," as Freud defined it. This is probably the first and loudest objection to what I've called Recognition. And the accusation of confirmation bias quickly comes to the fore. The accusation is that the claims of Christianity are so much imagined wishful thinking on the part of Christians, especially in the hope

of a blessed afterlife, that pulls the sting of death. And confirmation bias dictates that every bit of evidence is read to confirm
our prejudices. But to assume a materialistic point of view in
this case, *a priori*, is to lapse into circle logic. To the mind of the
materialist, such optimistic and self-condoling beliefs are doubt-
fully real, and laced with confirmation bias. We're not thinking
objectively if we approach the question of the truth or falsehood
of Christian faith, by starting with the assumption that it is false.

Lewis' response is to in detail show that as mythologies
go, Christianity is pretty dull and even off-putting compared to
everything else on the market of meaning-of-life philosophies,
as well as traditional mythologies. To Lewis, Norse Mythology
and not Christianity would be the thing he would believe if wish
fulfillment were his main criterion for choosing. Christianity is
an awkward affair with no heroes, giants, nor dragons, no "Twi-
light of the Gods," concerned with the uncomfortable business
of changing one's character to meet God's dreadfully high stan-
dard. Who would willingly choose that? Elsewhere Lewis writes,
"I didn't go to religion to make me happy. I always knew a bottle
of Port would do that. If you want a religion to make you feel
really comfortable, I certainly don't recommend Christianity."[1]
Just the thought that Christ was serious about the injunctions in
the Sermon on the Mount should send most people either flee-
ing, or severely editing or twisting their imagined Christianity
into some sort of strange cult and pseudo-Christianity that is
more reassuring and less demanding.

Sadly, that is often what happens. Christianity taken as the
gospels describe it, is supremely uncomfortable, and on first
look, extremely counter to our nature. It is no wonder that across
human history, people have rejected the humble and open-
hearted teachings that Jesus actually taught, for a tweaked version of Christianity, a religion of comfort, and one that justifies
their deeds of conquest, merciless acquisition, greed, and cruelty
in the name of God. And then, in entire dishonesty, such people
will call their bloody beliefs 'Christianity,' in a mockery of what

1. Lewis, *God in the Dock*, 48.

Christ actually taught. Live according to the Beatitudes? Who in their right mind would want to do *that*? Love my enemies? Give away my possessions? Do unto others as I want to be done by? Forget it! A bottle of Port is far more likely to induce temporary and rapid happiness. Or perhaps even a string of beers, or something harder.

As he pointed out in his allegorical *The Pilgrim's Regress*, the problem for Freudian thought is that in wielding the sword of the accusation of wish-fulfillment, that very sword is double-edged, and cuts both ways. So, if in a debate about confirmation bias, we're going to start swinging the sword of wish fulfillment, we're going to find that a lot of the cuts go against our own precious line of belief. Just because one is an atheist and a materialist doesn't mean that one is not possibly guilty of confirmation bias and the tendency toward wish fulfillment. How many people have desperately wished that God did not exist and that they were free of his demands? I am guessing the number would be in the billions.

Lewis in the talk then explores something he elsewhere calls "Evolutionism." He defines this as a long and developed myth that often goes with atheistic and materialistic beliefs. In the myth we see a long chain of development starting with primitive man, developed from his ape ancestors, and not only coming to master speech and basic technologies like the plow and agriculture, but also more and more sophisticated technologies. Over the millennia, humanity rises from its humble animal origins. Humanity, over time and with the aid of technology, masters nature. With the aid of psychology, humanity masters its own problems. In the end, this descendent of chimpanzees becomes a technological god that can travel the universe and do all things without the impediment of superstitions like religion.

Lewis calls this, with a wry smile. "Wellsianity"[2] as he felt that H.G. Wells was one of the more popular proponents of this notion. In fact, this Evolutionism has roots in the work of Matthew Arnold, John Stuart Mill, Thomas Henry Huxley, and other

2. Lewis, *Problem of Pain*, 79, footnotes.

critics and philosophers of the late Victorian period, before it finds full flower in post-1918 Modernism. And perhaps because Modernism itself, over a century later, today seems unable to die in the Western mindset, I still encounter writers who gush excitedly over the rapid technological changes of the Digital Age, as if paradise on earth were in the process of arriving before our very eyes. Expecting technology to correct the fatal flaws in human nature, which those 'backward' Christians call sin, is about as unrealistically optimistic as one can get. Haven't we learned that no tool we can invent cannot be, and will not fail to be perverted? What did our ancestors know about theft by hacking? Making war by computer invasion of the enemy's networks? Of the spreading of mad conspiracy theories on the net, that unite madmen that were once scattered? Of the spreading of child porn far beyond anyone's ability to stem the flow? Of using remote control cameras to shame and blackmail women, sometimes pushing them to suicide? But believe if you wish that technology will fix human nature. Go ahead. Good luck with that.

With Lewis, I have to suspect that this is far more wish-fulfillment than some humble woman kneeling in a church, confessing her sins, and trusting Christ for eternal life. Lewis loved images that portrayed contrary motion. Only the highest can reach to the lowest; only the infinite creator can reach down into the heart and soul of trillions of humans on an individual basis. And only those who can truly kneel will be lifted. Christ loved to speak in paradox. Surely such paradox is the sign of the Divine Hand that some of us might be able to see.

7.

On Obstinacy in Belief, Invisible Palaces, and the Numinous

IN ANOTHER ESSAY, LEWIS addresses the materialist claim that Christians believe on too little evidence. Lewis points out in some detail that the words "believe" and "belief" are used in different ways. There is a difference between "I believe I shall have a cup of tea" and "I believe in God." And furthermore, scientists when they talk about science, don't talk about 'belief' at all. They talk about hypothesis and evidence and conclusion.

Furthermore, Lewis defends the Christian belief that one must maintain faith even when there seems to be no evidence present that God is active and cares about the individual. Lewis likens this to a dog trusting an owner who releases the dog's paw from a trap by initially putting the paw in deeper before pulling it out altogether. And this is where what has been a dry argument up to this point starts to get interesting. For the Christian, belief is not simply a logical stance, or even a taken position given a certain amount of convincing evidence. Christian belief, Lewis argues, is a relationship upon which trust is slowly built. He writes:

> Our situation is rendered tolerable by two facts. One is
> that we seem to ourselves, besides the apparently con-
> trary evidence, to receive favourable evidence. Some
> of it is in the form of external events: as when I go to
> see a man, moved by what I felt to be a whim, and find
> he has been praying that I should come to him that
> day. Some of it is more like the evidence on which the
> mountaineer or the dog might trust his rescuer the res-
> cuer's voice, look, and smell. For it seems to us (though
> you, on your premises, must believe us deluded) that
> we have something like a knowledge-by-acquaintance
> of the Person we believe in, however imperfect and
> intermittent it may be. We trust not because "a God"
> exists, but because *this* God exists.[1]

This is probably as close as Lewis ever gets in attempting
a definition of Recognition. And though I consider Lewis the
Great Clarifier, even he has to dance around the thing. Granted,
he does a better job than I do, but that's to be expected.

There is one other place where Lewis, with the same sort
of characteristic transparency, describes the battle of belief and
doubt and the struggle to achieve what I have called Recognition, in his fiction. In *Till We Have Faces*, the main character,
Orual, loses her beloved little sister, Psyche, to a human sacrifice
in the mountains. Psyche is to become the Bride of the God,
also known as the Shadowbrute. When Orual ventures up the
mountain to bury the remains, she finds Psyche alive and well,
living across a river and in a grove that is filled with a sense of
the god's presence. Psyche lives in the god's palace, which Orual
cannot see. This sets up a unique experience where Orual must
judge whether Psyche is mad, delusional, or telling the truth.
Psyche calmly insists that she is the bride of an invisible god,
who is her husband and lover, but does not allow her to see his
face. Orual's emotions and contemplated action ricochet all over
as she tries to determine if she should kidnap Psyche, kill her
in mercy, or perhaps believe her. In the end, Orual goes back a
second time and convinces Psyche to look on the face of the god,

1. Lewis, *World's Last Night and Other Essays*, 24–25.

her husband, with a lamp. Psyche is caught and exiled, and the god appears to Orual and pronounces sentence on her as well.

Yet in terms of the concept of recognition, Orual in one of her emotional rambles considers for a short time the possibility that the palace really is there. During the first trip, as she is kneeling down on the far bank of the river, getting a drink with her hands, she begins to see the palace, though it is foggy and vague.[2] But her doubts overwhelm her. This makes her actually seeing the god on the second visit a bitter irony for her, for she has done all in the firm conviction that the god is either not there and Psyche is mad, or that the god is really just a bandit or a monster, and Psyche is deceived. Still, for the rest of the book, this partial vision of the palace and the clear vision and hearing of the speech of the god haunt her and make her sensitive to the thought that she has been wrong all along, that she has in fact fallen victim to confirmation bias, and that she has ruined Psyche's life as a result. However, the passages themselves are places where the narrator, Lewis, through his character, explores the state of mind as it battles over whether to accept this state I have called Recognition.

For Orual, not only can she not accept that she and Psyche live in different realities, but that this strange and holy thing, this presence of the god might actually be the truth. For how can she possess Psyche if she is competing with a god who is husband? When on the following morning, she kneels down by the river to drink, she sees the palace.[3] Lewis is very thorough here, not only reporting the sight of the palace, but the vagueness of it, and its propensity to disappear the moment Orual tries to even stand, and thereby begin a series of actions that allow her to verify the first vision. Here Lewis is showing us that belief must precede knowledge. That to cross the river and touch the palace before believing is not an option the god gives to Orual. And yet, the vision in the mist beckons her. But Lewis is also careful to show the reader that Orual herself does not want the palace to be real.

2. Lewis, *Till We Have Faces*, 25.

3. Lewis, *Till We Have Faces*, 132.

She wants some version of events that allows Orual to live with Psyche again, and as we find out later, to allow Orual to possess Psyche as she did when Psyche was a small child that Orual raised. As we read on into the novel, we find that this is the real issue. Orual wants to control her sister, to own her, and to be the only one Psyche loves. That is what keeps her from seeing the palace. Andrew Lazo has pointed out that Orual can only see the palace when she's *kneeling*. And Orual's punishment by the gods is to be made Queen of Glome and have total control of nearly everything in her world *but* Psyche, and to find that control is a false comfort, and leads only to misery. And more than just the control of Psyche, Orual wants to control all joy and beauty, and even something we vaguely call happiness in her life. It takes her the rest of the book to learn this bitter lesson.

Lewis often reiterates in fiction ideas that have surfaced in his essays. I have always believed that the ideas that Lewis puts forward in his essay "On Obstinacy in Belief" are fleshed out and paralleled in the invisible palace scenes in *Till We Have Faces*. But there is one other echo in Lewis' nonfiction. In the book *The Problem of Pain*, Lewis early on describes a term he borrows from Rudolph Otto, the "numinous." He defines this as something uncanny, a feeling all of us have had:

> It is "uncanny" rather than dangerous, and the special kind of fear it excites may be called Dread. With the Uncanny one has reached the fringes of the Numinous. . . . .This feeling may be described as awe, and the object which excites it as the *Numinous*.[4]

This is the sensation Orual has as she is seeing the invisible palace, and that she has again when she sees the god. And indeed, it is the sensation that Lewis has on the top of the bus. For all the materialist confirmation bias we have been taught in our culture since Descartes, many of us have had uncanny experiences that we cannot explain. Confirmed but unexplained miracles happen, in spite of the feverish energy to explain them away as being

4. Lewis, *Problem of Pain*, 3–4.

"unscientific." Lewis even gives us a picture of this, as Orual tries to explain what she saw in the god's valley to her Greek tutor, who is a materialist. With a thorough-going confirmation bias, he explains away Psyche's palace and god husband. But as Orual learns, her vision of the palace and the god were both true, and the Greek tutor's explaining away was the delusion.

This experience of the numinous was also Lewis' experience, this feeling the approach of something uncanny, something inexplicable at his own conversion. He speaks about it approaching him in almost a ghost-like way. Finally, he admits God is God, "the most dejected and reluctant convert in all England."[5] And this is at the heart of Recognition: God pursues us. Lewis here feels the "unrelenting approach." I suspect we all do, though something like 75% of us flee to any and every refuge and alternative. We really don't deserve it, and that fact does nothing to dissuade the Creator of the universe from pursuing us, each individually.

As young people like to say today: "Mind blown."

---

5. Lewis, *Surprised by Joy*, 228-9.

8.

From the Horse's Mouth and Psychological Studies

ACTUALLY, I BEG FORGIVENESS for being so coy myself, but up to this point I have not pointed out that I didn't really coin this use of the term "Recognition" with a capital R. In the last letter, Letter 31, of *The Screwtape Letters*, Screwtape, in a tone of disgust, is berating his nephew and narrating the experience of the "patient," who has been killed by a Luftwaffe bomb and has died and gone to be with Christ. This is a clear loss for the side of Hell, and Screwtape is letting his doomed nephew have an earful. More to our point, when that patient dies, he sees the meaning of everything, as well as clearly seeing his now-failed tempter. Lewis, interestingly, cites how the patient comes through an experience of joy that results in the Recognition of the person of Christ in the moment of death.

> But when he saw them he knew that he had always known them and realised what part each one of them had played at many an hour in his life when he had supposed himself alone, so that now he could say to them, one by one, not "Who *are* you?" but "So it was *you* all the time." . . . . The dim consciousness of friends about him which had haunted his solitudes from

infancy was now at last explained; that central music in every pure experience which had always just evaded memory was now at last recovered. *Recognition* [emphasis mine] made him free of their company almost before the limbs of his corpse became quiet.[1]

This fascinates me because Lewis here is clearly associating Recognition, with a capital R, with Joy. He actually links the two things.

But before I close this little chapter, I would like to revert to an image I'm sure I've already brought up: that is the image of Jill Pole with Aslan, where she tries to explain why she and Eustace Scrubb were calling to him. Aslan says, "You would not have called to me unless I had been calling to you."[2] This opens up both possibilities and questions. The whole question of predestination is here, but we've now covered that. The calling from both sides is effectively simultaneous, at least to the time-trapped human mind. And the full paradox here that Lewis addresses in the letters is laid out in a poetic image. But it's in the form of an assertion. Aslan makes no attempt to explain it to Jill in the way a philosopher might wish. You call because you were called. You were called because you call. Both things just are, in tandem, almost in a quantum relationship. Our minds try to apply a cause and effect, and all we gain is fruitless theological debates. As Lewis advised his correspondent, leave it alone. You cannot get to the bottom of it.

Having said that, I must address one other thing this late in the book: why haven't I brought in lots of psychological studies on the nature of belief? The reason is complex and yet in some sense, simple. Certainly, there are a wealth of such studies. But psychology, being a science, starts from a materialist assumption, that it will look only at that which can be measured and metered and observed. If we are not going to beg the question of the validity of belief, we have to go beyond that. If we proceed with the assumption that belief is not measurable by scientific experiment and therefore ruled out from the start, we have evaded

1. Lewis, *Screwtape Letters*, 158–59.
2. Lewis, *Silver Chair*, 12.

the issue in question. If belief in the supernatural is always in error, we may bring to the table lots of interesting information about how the brain works. Still, we will have gone on with a circle argument that precludes us from considering that belief is valid in something (God) that science cannot measure, meter, or observe in the material sense. We will be with those foolish cosmonauts who reported that they didn't see a huge old man with a white beard, like in the Michelangelo fresco, floating in Earth's orbit. Plus, as Lewis observed, we will have been restricting ourselves to "looking at" belief and not "looking along" belief.

In his essay "Meditation in a Toolshed," published in *God in the Dock*, Lewis describes an insight he got from Samuel Alexander, and found to be true in his own experience. He writes of seeing a shaft of light in a dark toolshed, that is coming through a crack. He notices that it is one experience to look *at* the shaft of light and yet another to place your eye in such a position as to look up the beam of light and see the sun outside, with leaves from a tree branch breaking up the light. This he calls "looking along" as opposed to "looking at." Scientific research only endeavors to "look at" phenomena. This book is about "looking along" the experience of belief. And this book does not accept the circle argument that in discussing the features of belief, we do not assume that belief is all delusional and futile, a materialist assumption. Our scientific methodology is committed to "looking at" things and dismissing "looking along."

Lewis believes that "looking along" an experience, being in the midst of it, is just as valid as "looking at" an experience. Indeed, it's a vast unproven assumption that lies under Materialism, that only observing something from the outside is objective. That idea itself is impossible to prove, which is why as a formal philosophy the materialist attitude, which was known as Logical Positivism, was abandoned after a short life. But Lewis' own illustration reveals his take on this. Looking along the sunbeam allows one to see outside the toolshed, and indeed all the way to the sun itself, our star. Looking at the same experience limits one to seeing a thin beam of light in a room of shadows.

Experiencing something, we've been taught, leads to delusion and confirmation bias. We can only "look at" things and collect data. Were that true, not only would this book not be worth writing, but all believing would be a delusion, and life itself a nihilistic and unknowable nightmare. The reader might accept that world view; I feel it is badly skewed. And it is probably a result of people not being able to believe in the supernatural because they feel that they have not conclusively experienced it. But that belongs in the next chapter.

9.

Back to Prophecy 101 and Why God Seems so Coy

Now that we've seen where C. S. Lewis stood on these issues, perhaps in a small way we can go back to that maddening passage in the Gospel of Luke, where the writer, probably Luke himself, conveys the story of the Risen Christ explaining what the passages about the Messiah from the *Tanakh* actually said about the Messiah, that they were expected to better understand. I would give a great deal to be able to jump into Dr Who's tardis and go back there with a microphone and a recorder, for that would be the ultimate midrash, the Divine Midrash. But no one did record it, with or without a tardis. *Sigh.* For other than seven events that I can think of, we have very little in terms of what Jesus is recorded to have said about how he himself specifically fulfilled prophecy. We have a lot of references by the narrators of the gospels on prophecies and Jesus, but as far as I can tell, only these seven where Jesus himself makes the interpretation.

1. We have Jesus' frequent references to himself as "The Son of Man" in multiple places, which identifies him with Messianic prophecies from the Book of Daniel.

2. We have Jesus declaring himself to be the fulfillment of Isaiah 61:1, in Luke 4:18, where he declares that the Spirit of the Lord is upon him, in the synagogue in Nazareth. As we saw above, his old friends and neighbors were unable to hear him.

3. In Matthew 11:14, Jesus tells us that his cousin, John the Baptist, was the Elijah to come before the Messiah, from Malachi 4:5–6.

4. We have the crisis moment, when Jesus tells Caiphas that he, Caiphas, will see the Son of Man on the right hand of God, which is a reference to Daniel 7. This is found in both Mark 14:62 and Matthew 26:64.

5. We have when Jesus in a confrontation with the Pharisees in Luke 20:17, refers to himself as the Cornerstone that men will stumble on from Psalm 118:22.

6. In Luke 24:44 Jesus tells his disciples, who are all together seeing him alive for the first time, after the Resurrection: "He said to them, 'This is what I told you while I was still with you: Everything must be fulfilled that is written about me in the Law of Moses, the Prophets and the Psalms.'"

7. And last, in Luke 22:36,37 Christ says to the Twelve, "But now if you have a purse, take it, and also a bag; and if you don't have a sword, sell your cloak and buy one. It is written: 'And he was numbered with the transgressors'; and I tell you that this must be fulfilled in me. Yes, what is written about me is reaching its fulfillment." This is from Isaiah 53:12.

There may be many places where Jesus quotes scripture, and perhaps someone might correct me, but I cannot think of any other places in the Gospels that Jesus authoritatively interprets what Christians call the Old Testament *in regards to himself*. He makes offhand references, even on the cross in Matthew 27:46 and Mark 15:34. But most the Gospel applications of Old Testament prophecy to Jesus are made by the narrators. I have often wondered if the tradition of these other passages being applied to Jesus starts with others reading the *Tanakh* and applying prophecy to Jesus. Or was what Jesus told Cleopas and Maybe-Luke at least in part remembered, and passed down to the Gospel writers as authoritative tradition by the church? I strongly suspect that this latter scenario is what happened, and that the confidence of New Testament writers in their readings of Jewish scripture pointing to Jesus as the Messiah are based on his own interpretations.

But that's my guess and not an established fact. And questions like this one are just the beginning of the fire-swamp of Messianic prophecy. I'll give you a small taste of some of the controversies. The principal problem is that none of these Old Testament prophecies are anything like clear and unambiguous proof-texts. As with the prophecy in Isaiah 61:1, the words that Jesus quotes are mixed in with other things the prophet is saying that are clearly about the era that Isaiah lived in. The entire passage reads:

> 1 The spirit of the Lord God is upon me
>   because the Lord has anointed me;
> he has sent me to bring good news to the oppressed,
>   to bind up the brokenhearted,
> to proclaim liberty to the captives
>   and release to the prisoners,
> 2 to proclaim the year of the Lord's favor
>   and the day of vengeance of our God,
>   to comfort all who mourn,
> 3 to provide for those who mourn in Zion—
>   to give them a garland instead of ashes,
> the oil of gladness instead of mourning,
>   the mantle of praise instead of a faint spirit.
> They will be called oaks of righteousness,
>   the planting of the Lord, to display his glory.
> 4 They shall build up the ancient ruins;
>   they shall raise up the former devastations;
> they shall repair the ruined cities,
>   the devastations of many generations.
> 5 Strangers shall stand and feed your flocks;
>   foreigners shall till your land and dress your vines,

6 but you shall be called priests of the Lord;
    you shall be named ministers of our God;
you shall enjoy the wealth of the nations,
    and in their riches you shall glory.
7 Because their shame was double
    and dishonor was proclaimed as their lot,
therefore in their land they shall possess a double portion;
    everlasting joy shall be theirs.
8 For I, the Lord, love justice,
    I hate robbery and wrongdoing;
I will faithfully give them their recompense,
    and I will make an everlasting covenant with them.
9 Their descendants shall be known among the nations
    and their offspring among the peoples;
all who see them shall acknowledge
    that they are a people whom the Lord has blessed.
10 I will greatly rejoice in the Lord;
    my whole being shall exult in my God,
for he has clothed me with the garments of salvation;
    he has covered me with the robe of righteousness,
as a bridegroom decks himself with a garland
    and as a bride adorns herself with her jewels.
11 For as the earth brings forth its shoots
    and as a garden causes what is sown in it to spring up,
so the Lord God will cause righteousness and praise
    to spring up before all the nations.

Christ in the synagogue only reads and refers to verses 1 and 2. Yet, Christ elsewhere refers to himself as "the bridegroom."[1] Can we then assume verse 10 applies to him as well? Verses 3 through 7 at least on the surface level apply to Jews returning to Israel in something like an ideal messianic age. Can they be applied to roughly 30 CE, when Christ reads these words in the synagogue in Nazareth? One of the great points of confusion is this telescoping of prophecy concerning Christ's time on earth, and Christ's second coming. It is never clearly spelled out which time a given prophecy on the Messiah is addressing, his life between 6 CE and 33–39 CE, or in the future Second Coming.

1. Mark 2 :19.

It is this kind of ambiguity in Old Testament prophecy that makes us bridle a little at the idea that Christ was scolding Cleopas and Maybe-Luke for not having all this matter crystal clear. Just looking at Isaiah 61 alone, we have possible prophetic fulfillment in both present and Second Coming, and no clear indication which is which. Plus, in other instances, both present and future are invoked. The most well-known example of this is the prophecy given in Matthew 1: 22-23, where the narrator assures us that the prophecy in Isaiah 7 refers to the birth of Christ. But in context, the passage is part of a narrative in which Isaiah is before the King of Judah, Ahaz, assuring him in the Name of Yahweh, that the Samarian-Syrian threat of attack will come to nothing. It reads:

> Again the Lord spoke to Ahaz, saying, "Ask a sign of the Lord your God; let it be deep as Sheol or high as heaven." But Ahaz said, "I will not ask, and I will not put the Lord to the test." Then Isaiah said, "Hear then, O house of David! Is it too little for you to weary mortals that you weary my God also? Therefore the Lord himself will give you a sign. Look, the young woman is with child and shall bear a son and shall name him Immanuel. He shall eat curds and honey by the time he knows how to refuse the evil and choose the good. For before the child knows how to refuse the evil and choose the good, the land before whose two kings you are in dread will be deserted. The Lord will bring on you and on your people and on your ancestral house such days as have not come since the day that Ephraim departed from Judah—the king of Assyria.

The pivotal verse, 14, in context of the passage, makes zero reference to the Messiah. It's all about Judah not being conquered by the Northern Kingdom (aka, Ephraim, Samaria, Israel, the 10 tribes) in alliance with Syria. Being able to clearly see that as a messianic prophecy would be beyond my skills. But as I have argued above, this is not a matter of discerning proof-texts, which is the way most people I've encountered tend to read such things. That's why I believe that if Christ was gently scolding Cleopas and Maybe-Luke, it was not for mistakes in correct interpretations of proof-texts, but for lacking a spirit tuned to belief, lacking some sense of Recognition.

And, more importantly, this is why I have maintained that an ability to believe and discern prefigures belief. For someone tuned to Jesus of Nazareth and what he said and taught, this passage will pop out like an Agatha Christie clue. It may be more of an echo than a proof-text, but then in Recognition, we are given a grace to understand even faint echoes. For someone looking for something undeniable, some sort of glaring proof-text, they will only be disappointed. Yet, for all the truth of that assertion, I'm still a bit leery about doubting the application of logic to the Old Testament when I think how decisively Jesus crushed the Sadducee argument about life after death with an unambiguous quote about Yahweh saying that "I am the God of Abraham, Isaac, and Jacob" in the present tense. We may think of Spock or Sherlock Holmes as the ultimate logicians, but the shrewdness of Christ's responses to the Pharisees and Sadducees demonstrates that he had an excessively quick and logical mind, and he seems to expect his followers to come up to his mark. Yet, as tangled up as many people get over these sorts of matters, I don't think this is what really challenges our belief and our ability to recognize Christ when he calls to us. And I say that while sadly acknowledging that it is not hard at all in this day and age, to find some Christian having a life-long OCD episode trying to pin down all the prophecies and proof-texts in the New and Old Testaments in a neat but complex systematic grid. Such people usually feel themselves called by God to "correct" everyone else and teach their system as if it were the very Gospel. If I may loosely paraphrase Lewis, they have built their God a magnificent temple, only to find that God has flown. Most often that doesn't stop them from trying to convince everyone else that their huge effort is correct and not a waste of time. Again, it comes back to me, "The wind [Spirit] blows where it chooses, and you hear the sound of it, but you do not know where it comes from or where it goes. So it is with everyone who is born of the Spirit."[2] Lewis once said that trying to systematize the teachings of Christ was like trying to "bottle a sunbeam." Still, far too many people continue to try, and build up towers of interpretation in this vain sort of temple-building, using primarily the Old Testament and the Book of Revelation .

But I think our real question, that all of us who have ever considered the claims of Christ, have burning in our breast is: *why does God play so 'hard to get'? Why is the Eternal so very coy? Why does God give no sign when demanded or requested?* Now, I realize that my claim to this being a common thought is impossible for me to know, as I cannot read the mind of others, but I'm pretty sure I'm right on this one. Yes, having come this far, we can see that all talk of predestination is an illusion of an anthropomorphized God who is locked in time as we are. And we see that universalism in the strict sense violates free will. And perhaps by this time, you have conceded that my argument for the existence of some paradoxical middle state, that I have called Recognition, exists out there, and always has.

But our deeper inclination is to wonder why God doesn't put on a real big show for us, especially when our faith is feeling thin. I know I have been frustrated by knowing those who scoff because they've seen no gigantic divine hand like the one in Daniel 5, or a white-bearded old man, floating on the clouds as in the Michelangelo fresco, ordering any part of this life or universe, or so they say. And it's a good question. However, as Lewis points out in the opening of his book, *Miracles,* seeing is not believing. There he tells of the one person he knows who claims to have seen a ghost, and that that person does not believe that it was a ghost.[3] This goes back to confirmation bias, and the fact that confirmation bias can work both ways. The person indisposed to believe would refuse to believe in the face of undeniable miracles. The materialist is quite as capable of confirmation bias as the theist.

2. John 3:8.
3. Lewis, *Miracles,* 3.

Sure, there have been moments when the Divine has broken through with an impressive display of power or personal presence: Moses parting the Sea of Reeds, Jacob's vision and wrestle with God, and the many other Old Testament miracles that have been recorded. But people doubt old documents, so those as testimony are swept away as surely as the Egyptian chariots. Like Lewis's woman who saw a ghost, we won't believe what we haven't seen with our own eyes, and often not even that.

I truly suspect that on a subconscious level, many of us actually *are* waiting for that giant hand to write on the wall. We want to be able to touch and see an overwhelming God as surely as we can touch another person, or a wall, or our car. Better yet, would God kindly let us read him on our instruments, or let us analyze his divine DNA, so that we can feel we've got a handle on him. That is what the Russian cosmonauts were looking for: a god who showed up on instruments, benignly floating in Earth's orbit. Even putting such absurdities aside, the answer is always, no.

Still, many of us have experienced unexplained miracles ourselves, but those are all too conveniently explained away by doubters citing medical science or psychology. Our post-Enlightenment confirmation bias renders us most likely to explain away everything we cannot understand. Still, many of us hunger for some proof, some undeniable display of divine power and presence.

Some forms of Christianity like to emphasize the Second Coming with a Hollywood level of horror, disaster, and just plain drama. If we believe at all, we are very likely to wish Our Lord would prove himself to the world and make our task a lot easier. What if the Creator just showed up and shouted "Everyone out of the pool!" like a summer-camp lifeguard? We hunger for God to be that assertive at times, and physically and obviously present; he doesn't do it. And for all the shouting in the last 60 years about an imminent Second Coming, it hasn't happened yet. But those of us who do believe at times wish God would just *get loud*. That would show all those scoffers and doubters!

But he doesn't operate like that at all. Instead, when he was here, he told parables and confessed that he did so to obscure his meaning for many.[4] He kept saying 'Let him who has ears, hear.' This sounds rudely exclusive at first hearing. But I believe Our Lord knew from the start that some would never listen and never believe. Was he right? In John 10:24, the Pharisees demand he tell them if he is the Messiah. His answer is basically, 'I already did, but you cannot believe, because you're not of my sheep.' Recognition again. This may seem rude and dismissive, but if so, Jesus had good cause. The Pharisees indeed saw many miracles, and except for two exceptions that we know of,[5] they all of them disbelieved, so that Jesus calls them "blind guides." This is why Jesus tells them "I already told you," implying 'Why do you keep asking when I've already answered you?' In fact, he knew that most people would never listen and never believe. The Parable of the Sower I have often thought to be indicative of God's expectations for the human race. First, recall that in Christ's parable, he mentions the sower spreading seed four times and being successful only once. Think of that: God incarnate arrived to perform his mission expecting it to have something like a 75% failure rate. How many of us could stomach that sort of expectation, and still make a try to carry out a plan? Would you fly in a jet that had a projected 75% failure rate?

When Jesus tells the parable of the sown seed, out of four tries, only one try lands on fertile ground.[6] Not what I'd call great expectations. This gets us back into predestination again, but we've already addressed that. Notice also that Jesus does miracles when people have faith, and is inhibited in this when he is in Nazareth, where his friends and neighbors doubt him.

Yet, the most clear reason for this 'coyness', this low expectation approach, this absence of shouting, this use of what has been called the "still, small voice," is intentional. The reason can be seen when Jesus, in John chapter 12, in the view of multiple

4. Matthew 13:10–17.
5. Nicodemus and Joseph of Arimathea.
6. Matthew 13:1–16.

witnesses and a group of Pharisees, raises a man who is four days dead, from the grave. If *that's* not getting loud and putting on a big show, I don't know what is. And just what is the response to this impressive show of miraculous power? The Pharisees conspire how to kill him, and the risen man as well, so that they can claim it was all a hoax.[7] I've always thought it odd that it didn't occur to them that you could not successfully kill a man who has power over death. But they had severe confirmation bias, and were certain that it all was a hoax, mainly because it was not what they wanted Yahweh to be like.

I am truly convinced that no amount of spectacular and miraculous show would change most people's minds. If God shouted, and raised dead people right and left, clearing out the cemeteries, most people would close their ears and eyes, and find some way to explain it away. In this sense, we're almost all like the Pharisees in that we are so committed to our own preferred version of reality, that we will betray the very teachings we make a big deal about defending, in order to preserve our delusion.

Thus, the answer to the question is that God doesn't waste the effort. If there were spiritual benefit for a St. Maria Faustina Kowalska to see Jesus face to face, Jesus apparently will make the effort. When the Pharisees come to demand a miracle from Jesus, he refuses, knowing full well that it would be as useless to them as the witnessing of the resurrection of Lazarus.[8] Let he who has ears to hear, and let he who has eyes to see, so see. But the Almighty ain't putting on a show for you-all to merely scoff at. Put simply, God incarnate doesn't care to waste time on those who refuse to believe under any circumstances.

For me, this goes a long way to explain Recognition, even if I struggle to define it. There are those of us who by free will choose the Love of God. He foreknew it, but it wasn't predestined because God is outside time. So, speaking more accurately, he simply knows it. As I said above, God only sees in the present tense. For those who love him, we are those who both chose

7. John 12: 9–11.
8. Matthew 12:38–39.

freely and were freely chosen. A paradox, no doubt, but that is the case. And it is given to us to recognize the voice of the Shepherd.[9] This is a grace, mysterious and inexplicable, as well as incomprehensible. Let she or he who has ears . . . and eyes, hear and see. Let she or he who does not . . . well, they're not going to get a show, big or small. The Almighty does not waste effort, and what he purposes comes to pass regardless of our best efforts to mess it up, and even if the grant of free will makes the Divine effort only 25% effective. It is so because in amongst all the things that could mean, he purposes to delegate to us the power of free will, including the will to be blind and deaf. Lewis once said of Hell that its doors were locked from the inside. So also here. We are still multi-millions of us in this 21st century world, fully capable of seeing a man plucked back from four days dead, and *still* refusing to believe. Most of us are like the Pharisees. It is a part of our choice. But if somewhere in us is that morsel, that small crumb of willingness to believe, then somehow by the mystery of grace, outside of the confines of rude time, we are chosen in the moment that we freely choose. It doesn't feel like that though; it feels more like waking up and saying to he who calls to us, "Oh! It's *you*. Well, that's alright then."

Lewis describes this first moment of his own personal recognition in *Surprised by Joy*, when he is riding home on the upper level of a bus. He described the feeling like something in him was melting, and that though he was free to choose, there didn't seem to be any other choice.[10]

As noted above, Lewis in the Narnia series portrays this profound moment also in another way, in *The Silver Chair* when Jill Pole says that she and Eustace Scrubb had been calling to someone. Aslan replies "You would not have called to me unless I had been calling to you."[11] I'd call the two things simultaneous, but that would be to imply that they are inside time. As I have already said, it's a paradox and a mystery, but, as Lewis wrote to

9. John 10: 27–28.

10. Lewis, *Surprised by Joy*, 224–225.

11. Lewis, *Silver Chair*, 19.

his correspondent, I think it's better to rejoice gratefully than to puzzle one's head trying to work it out.

To reiterate, ultimately the only answer to this paradox is Christ's own words. In John 10: 27, 28 it reads:

> My sheep hear my voice. I know them, and they follow me. I give them eternal life, and they will never perish. No one will snatch them out of my hand.

Epilogue

A Place for Humility and Wonder

So, WHAT ARE MY conclusions about that remarkable moment in human history where God incarnate gently scolded his followers for not getting what I have called the Agatha Christie type clues in the Jewish sacred writings, that were obscure at best? First, I want to avoid at all costs being one of those intense and righteous persons who go at the Bible like it were a mysterious, supernatural codebook, like in a Dan Brown novel, or some of the books in the last few decades which "decoded" the Bible to give an exact reading of the Second Coming. I think the OCD approach is not only mentally unhealthy, but misguided. And beneath all of it is the vast temptation to Pride, the worst of all sins, Pride that *you*, you know the exact date and time of the Second Coming, or have the *exact* and *correct* version of Christian theology, unlike the poor, misguided rest of humanity, who should be bowing to your superior spirituality and intellect. The Greeks called this attitude "hubris" and knew that it inevitably led to a bad end. Remember Oedipus and Creon?

If God Incarnate chose to be humble, those of us who are unworthy to even untie his sandals should not get a big head.

And if the temptation to such self-destructive hubris weren't enough, the person who works feverishly in an OCD fashion to systematize Christianity is incapable of receiving it like a child.[1] St Paul reminds us that any achievement that doesn't have love at its heart, is ultimately futile.[2]

But then, I believe the current fad for conspiracy theories and the lust for mysterious puzzles, when applied to the Bible and dogma, has another sort of temptation. If we are locked in a fascinating quest for the Truth about the exact date of the Second Coming (never mind that Christ said we can't know it), or some sort of "Bible code," or some doctrine which we firmly believe is necessary to be a true Christian, we transform ourselves. Or rather, we imagine that we transform ourselves. The offer of the excitement creates a kind of lust to leave behind the mundane world and follow the mystery and conspiracy. If we can discard the complex facts for simple generalizations, and define just who the Bad Guys are (our opponents, no doubt) and the Good Guys (us, of course), our uneventful and unexciting lives become an adventure. We become Indiana Jones or Lara Croft against the Sinners who don't agree with our meticulous, OCD reading of some prophecy in the Bible or some dogma that we champion. Our cause becomes Holy and we are the Good Guys fighting evil.

What we lose sight of when we cave in to such simplistic and dubious thinking, is our own sins. The awareness of our own flawed nature quite goes out the window. We become the all-virtuous action heroes in our own minds, and set out to destroy the Forces of Darkness. It not only gives us a false sense of self-righteousness, but it also makes our lives exciting in a self-deceptive way. We have projected ourselves into our own imagined action movie, in which we star.

For we wouldn't want to risk laying our egos aside and letting God work on our hearts in a fight against our real enemies: our pride, our selfishness, our callousness to the pain of others, and all the parade of our sins. Being the OCD action hero allows us to sweep away any memory of our sins, throw the burden of

1. Matthew 18:3.
2. 1 Corinthian 13:1–3.

evil in the world on the imagined Bad Guys, and stride proudly onward in blindness to any evil we end up causing. I believe it was this kind of thinking that led to the Holocaust in Germany, when the German church was persuaded to pass judgement on the "Bad Guys," who happened to be the Jews. It was this kind of thinking which led to the Inquisition. It is a deceptive and addicting form of evil, to focus on your own interpretation and your own self-righteousness. And it is far more attractive and deadly than opioid addiction. I think Lewis had it right: if you think you are not proud, it is a certain sign that you are.

Well then, just how do we figure out the incident at Emmaus? The correct reading of Scripture? Who is right in the denominational debate? Can I be sure of anything at all and not fall into the trap of self-righteousness?

The answer is never easy. But again I will point out two principles.

One: the Spirit blows where it will. If your reading of dogma and scripture has God neatly pigeon-holed and defined, and oddly there are *still* those people who don't agree with you, and yet they somehow seem to flourish, then maybe you need to adopt some Negative Capability of your own. Jesus did *not* say that you are my friends if you totally understand everything concerning faith. He said you are my friends if you act on what I've taught you.[3] Maybe consider breaking down and putting your system charts of theology aside. Working in a ministry to the poor might not be exciting or fun, but it's clearly an act of following Christ. Start there and leave your mind open to learn something you had not logicked out yourself. The ways of God are beyond human understanding. Accept that fact and just act on Christ's actual teachings, and I think you'll not only learn more, but you'll find that much of what you thought important was only so much straw, to paraphrase St Thomas Aquinas.

Two: Along with the humility of being open to learning through acting on Christ's teaching, abandon the temptation to see yourself as some sort of action hero for God. What you do in

---

3. John 15:14.

this life may yet benefit many and glorify God. But it never happens when you are planning it out yourself. You've got to let go of the controls and move forward in small steps in faith. Remember he said "Without me you can do nothing."[4] Then a kind of Recognition happens, and you not only become transformed in ways you could not have foreseen—much to your surprise, you see things clearly for the very first time, that were right in front of your eyes all the time. This is what happened to Cleopas and Maybe-Luke. When God speaks, he usually uses his "still, small voice" and we hear it out of nowhere as it were. If that voice tells you to go conquer and force others to think or believe a certain way, to follow in *your* teaching, you can be sure it's your ego or your fear, or both, talking. God, when he does talk to us, like Christ on the road to Emmaus, he opens our eyes to things we had not thought of, usually with a gentle scolding on how blind we have been. That's the real lesson of the incident on the road to Emmaus. When God speaks to us, one of the sure ways to know it was him was that what you feel you've been commanded to do was one, against your ego, two, against your understanding, and three, it was about love. If it doesn't meet those three tests, you are on your way to fancying yourself to be Indiana Jones, Lara Croft, or Robert Langdon. If you feel your life is so dull and meaningless, that you need to add this element of action, adventure, and romance, you need to retreat and to find what God really wants for you and from you. And don't be surprised if it's more difficult, seemingly boring, and less adventurous than the delusion that you're starring in a Dan Brown movie.

Steer away from any and all generalizations. Turn on your Negative Capability, and slow down and silence yourself to listen. Don't be impatient. When you least expect it, in the depths of even the worst despair, some apparent stranger will walk with you and set your mind on fire with what she or he reveals to you about you and the meaning of your life. And just perhaps, when you break bread with her or him, you might recognize the Master.

4. John 15:5.

Works Cited

Clowney, Edmund P. *The Unfolding Mystery: Discovering Christ in the Old Testament.* 2nd ed. P&R, 2013.

Holwerda, David E. *Jesus and Israel: One Covenant or Two?* Eerdmans, 1995.

Karelius, Brad. *Desert Spirit Places: the Sacred Southwest.* Wipf and Stock, 2018.

Keats, John. *Letters of John Keats.* ed Robert Giddings. Oxford UP, 1979.

Lewis, C.S. *All My Road Before Me: The Diary of C.S. Lewis 1922–1927.* ed Walter Hooper. Harcourt, 1991.

———. *The Allegory of Love.* Oxford: Oxford UP, 1936.

———. *The Collected Letters II.* Harper San Francisco, 2004

———. *The Collected Letters III.* Harper San Francisco, 2007.

———. *Christian Reflections.* ed Walter Hooper. Grand Rapids: Eerdmans, 1967.

———. *Christian Reunion and Other Essays.* ed. Walter Hooper, Fount, 1990.

———. *The Discarded Image.* Cambridge: Cambridge UP, 1964.

———. *English Literature in the Sixteenth Century Excluding Drama.* Clarendon, 1954.

———. "Equality." *The Spectator* CLXXI (27 Aug 1943) 192.

———. *An Experiment in Criticism.* Cambridge: Cambridge UP, 1961.

———. *Fern-seeds and Elephants: and other Essays on Christianity.* Fount, 1975.

———. *God in the Dock: Essays on Theology and Ethics.* Grand Rapids: Eerdmans, 1970.

———. *The Great Divorce.* New York: Collier, 1946.

———. *The Horse and His Boy.* New York: Macmillan, 1954.

———. *The Last Battle.* New York: Macmillan, 1956.

———. *Letters C.S. Lewis Don Giovanni Calabria.* Trans Martin Moynihan. Servant, 1998.

———. *Letters of C.S. Lewis: Revised and Enlarged Edition.* ed Walter Hooper. Harcourt, 1988.

———. *Letters to Malcolm: Chiefly on Prayer.* Harcourt, 1963.

———. *The Letters of C.S. Lewis to Arthur Greeves.(1914–1963).* ed. Walter Hooper. Collier, 1979.

———. *The Lion, the Witch and the Wardrobe.* New York: Macmillan, 1950.

———. *The Magician's Nephew.* New York: Macmillan, 1955.

———. "Membership." In *The Weight of Glory.* London: Macmillan, 1963.

———. *Miracles.* London: Macmillan, 1960.

———. *On Stories and Other Essays on Literature.* Walter Hooper, ed.

——— and EMW Tillyard. *The Personal Heresy: A Controversy.* Edited by Joel Heck. Concordia, 2008. Reprint.

———. "On the Transmission of Christianity." God in the Dock. Grand Rapids: Eerdmans, 1970.

———. *Poems.* Ed. Walter Hooper. Fount, 1994

———. *A Preface to Paradise Lost.* Oxford: Oxford UP, 1961.

———. *Prince Caspian.* New York: Macmillan, 1951.

———. *Reflections on the Psalms.* Harcourt, 1963.

———. *Selected Literary Essays.* Walter Hooper, ed. Cambridge UP, 1969.

———. *The Silver Chair.* Macmillan, 1953.

———. *The Screwtape Letters.*Collins, 1942.

———. *Spenser's Images of Life.* Alastair Fowler, ed. Cambridge UP, 1967.

———. *Studies in Medieval and Renaissance Literature.* Cambridge UP, 1966.

———. *Studies in Words.* Cambridge UP, 1960.

———. *Surprised by Joy.* Harcourt, 1955.

———. *Till We Have Faces.* Harcourt, 1956.

———. *The Voyage of the Dawn Treader.* Macmillan, 1952.

———. "The World's Last Night." *The World's Last Night and Other Essays.* Harcourt, 1952.

———. *The Weight of Glory and Other Addresses.* Edited by Walter Hooper. 1980.

Mowinckel, Sigmund. *He That Cometh: The Messiah Concept in the Old Testament & Later Judaism.* Eerdman's, 2005 (1956).

Prothero, James. *Sunbeams and Bottles: the Theology, Thought, and Reading of C. S. Lewis.* Winged Lion, 2022.

Rydelnik, Michael, and Edwin Blum, eds. *The Moody Handbook of Messianic Prophecy: Studies and Expositions of the Messiah in the Old Testament.* Moody, 2019.

* 9 7 9 8 3 8 5 2 5 8 3 2 1 *